1. Here are the two Hebrew letters you've learned: BET בּ & VET ב

2. Write the letter with the saying sound of B _____.

3. Write the letter with the saying sound of V _____.

4. Whenever you see this letter בּ you sound it _____.

5. Whenever you see this letter ב you sound it _____.

6. The vowel AY as in DAY is written _____.

7. To read the sound BAY, we combine the BET בּ and the vowel

   AY as in DAY ֵ so: בֵּ

   Practice writing a whole row of בֵּ beginning here ——————————————————————

   ——— ——— ——— ——— ——— ——— ——— ——— ——— ——— ——— ———

   Now do a row with the sound of VAY.

   ——— ——— ——— ——— ——— ——— ——— ——— ——— ——— ——— ———

8. Read this line aloud, slowly at first, then try it increasing your speed with each reading. (When there is no vowel just give the saying sound of the letter.)

   בֵּ ב בּ ב ב בֵּ בֵּ ב בּ בֵ ב בֵ ←

NEW LETTERS AND VOWELS:

‍	‍	ד	ר ←
AH	AH	D	R

LETTERS AND VOWELS YOU KNOW:

בּ	ב
AY	B	V

---

1. This ר is RAYSH. *Head* This ד is DAHLET. *Doorway* Under each letter below write its saying sound.

ר   ר   ר   ד   ר   ד   ר   ד   ד ←

_____ _____ _____ _____ _____ _____ _____ _____ _____

2. We'll combine the ר and ד with the vowel ‥ AY. You fill in the sounds.

(Remember when you use English letters, always write them in the order you are accustomed to: DAY and RAY.)

רֵ   דֵ   רֵ   דֵ   דֵ   רֵ ←

_____ _____ _____ _____ _____ _____

3. Now we'll combine the new vowels ‍ and ‍ AH as in OOMPAH.

   a. This letter and vowel  are read as _____.

   b. This letter and vowel are read as _____.

   c. This letter and vowel are read as _____.

   d. This letter and vowel are read as _____.

4. Match these two columns.

   RAY ( )   (1) בּ

   BAH ( )   (2) בָ

   DAY ( )   (3) רֵ

   VAH ( )   (4) דֵ

5. Let's try combining and reading two syllables.

   This reads RAH RAH   רַ רָ ←

   This reads _____ רַ בֵּ ←

   This reads _____ דָ בֵּ ←

6. One of these sounds reads VAH BAY. Which one? (   )

   דֵ בָ   בָ בֵ   בֵּ רֵ   רֵ בָ   דַ דֵ ←
   (e)   (d)   (c)   (b)   (a)

7. The sounds BAY RAH are written   _____ _____ ←
                (1)   (2) (use —)   (2)   (1)

   The sounds DAH BAH are written   _____ _____
               (1)   (2) (use both vowels)   (2)   (1)

   The sounds VAY DAH are written   _____ _____
               (1)   (2) (use either vowel)   (2)   (1)

8. Try to read these now, speedily but accurately.

   בֵּרַ דָבּ רַכ דֵר בָ בַּ ←

   (Have someone 'time' your reading when you know it well.)

9. You know that to make a Hebrew word we combine syllables and read them together. Here are three Hebrew words.

   a. The word רַ בּ reads_____.

   b. The word בַּ ר reads_____.

   c. The word דַ בֵּ ר reads_____.

LETTERS AND VOWELS YOU KNOW:

AH   AH   AY   D   R   V   B

---

1. SHEEN is written this way_____.

2. SEEN is written this way_____.

3. To read the sound SAY, we add the vowel AY **..** to the  so:

   Write a line of ⱱ beginning here _____

   _____

   Now try SHAY ⱱ _____

   _____

   How about a row of SAH _____

   _____

4. Fill in the correct vowel to complete each sound.

   SAY   SHAH   SAH   SHAY

   ⱱ   ⱱ   ⱱ   ⱱ ←
                (use other vowel) (either vowel)

5. Ready for some practice reading aloud? But no mistakes, please; remember accuracy is most important.

   Try it again doing it more quickly.

6. We'll try two syllables now. See how quickly you can read these.

(Bit of a tongue-twister, wasn't it?)

7. These are the letters you know. We'll write their saying sounds, you write their names.

Saying Sounds	V	R	S	B	D	SH

Names _____ _____ _____ _____ _____ _____

8. Under each letter and vowel write its sound.

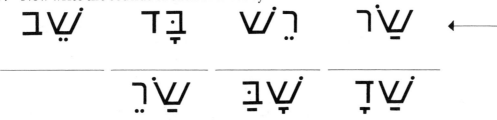

_____ _____ _____ _____

9. Now write the sounds of each of these syllables.

שֶׁב   דָּ בֶ   רֶ שְׁ   שֹׁר   ←

_____ _____ _____ _____

שְׁר   שֵׁ בָּ   שָׁד

_____ _____ _____

10. Shall we try some speed-reading again?

בֶ   דֶ   דָ   בֶּ   שָׁ   שֵׁ   רֶ   בֶּ   דֵ   ←

11. Practice reading double syllables now.

בֶ דַ   שָׁ דֶ   רֵ שַׁ   שַׁ בֵּ   שַׁ רֶ   ←

5

You've learned six letters and three vowels. See how quickly you can read them. And more than that, see how well you can read the Hebrew words at the bottom of the page.

1   ב ב כ ב כ ב ב ב ב ב ב כ

2   ר ד ר ד ר ד ד ד ר ד ר ר

3   שׁ שׁ שׁ שׁ שׁ שׁ שׁ שׁ שׁ שׁ שׁ שׁ

4   שׁ ר שׁ ד ב ר שׁ ד ב ר שׁ שׁ

5   ֵ ֶ ָ ֵ ֶ ָ ֵ ֶ ָ ֵ ֶ ֵ

6   בֶּ רֵ דָ בֵּ שֶ שָ שֵ בַ דָ רָ בָּ דָ

7   שָׁר רַ־שָׁ רָב שֵׁב שַׁב

8   שָׁשׁ שָׁר שַׁר דַב דָּב

meat	sit!	"R"	speak!	
בָּשָׂר	שֵׁב	רֵשׁ	דַּבֵּר	9

hail	six	broke	explained	
בָּרָד	שֵׁשׁ	שָׁבַר	דָּרַשׁ	10

NEW LETTERS:

תּ ת
T   T

LETTERS YOU KNOW:

שׂ שׁ ד ר בּ בּ

S   SH   D   R   V   B

VOWELS YOU KNOW:

ָ   ַ   ֵ
AH AH AY

1. TAHV is written תּ and has the saying sound of _____.

2. TAHV also is written this way ת and still has the saying sound of _____.

3. The three vowels you've learned are:

    ֵ AY as in _____

    ַ AH as in _____

    ָ AH as in _____

4. Practice reading these vowels aloud, beginning here ⟶

    ָ   ֵ   ָ   ַ   ֵ   ָ   ֵ   ַ   ַ   ָ ⟵

5. Now read these vowels combined with this תּ TAHV and this ת TAHV.

    תֵּ   תֵ   תַ   תָ   תַּ   תֵּ   תֵ   תָ   תָּ

6. Under each Hebrew letter below, write its name.

    ר   בּ   תּ   שׁ ⟵

_____ _____ _____ _____

7. This time we'll give you the name of each letter, you write the Hebrew letter.

    TAHV   SEEN   DAHLET   VET ⟵

_____ _____ _____ _____

8. This letter and vowel שַׂ reads _____.

9. This letter and vowel ךְ reads _____.

10. This letter and vowel דֻ reads _____.

11. This letter and vowel בַ reads _____.

12. Match these columns.

TAY ( )   (1) תָ

TAH ( )   (2) בֵ

VAH ( )   (3) תֵּ

SAH ( )   (4) שַׂ

13. Practice reading aloud each of these syllables.

בֵ רְ בָ דָ בֶ תֵּ בְּ שֵׁ ←

14. Read these phrases slowly the first time. Then read them again increasing your speed. But remember accuracy is more important than speed.

דָּ רְשָׁ בַּת תֵּבֶ שֵׁבָ שָׁבָ ←

15. Here are several Hebrew words. One of them reads SHAH-BAHT—SABBATH. Copy that word in the space provided.

שַׁבָּת בַּת דָּבָר שַׂר ←

This is the word for SABBATH _____.

8

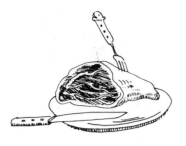

Here's a review of all the letters and vowels you know. Say out loud the name of each letter in the first four rows. Then continue to read. See if you can find the Hebrew word for SABBATH.

1 בּ תּ תּ בּ תּ תּ בּ תּ בּ תּ

2 שׁ שׁ שׁ שׁ שׁ שׁ שׁ שׁ שׁ שׁ

3 ר ר ד ר ד ד ד ד ר ד

4 תּ תּ בּ ד שׁ ר תּ בּ תּ שׁ ד ר תּ

5 ׁ ׁ ׁ ָ ׁ ־ ָ ׁ ־ ׁ ָ ־ ׁ ־ ָ ־ ׁ ָ

6 תַּ תָּ תַּ תָ תַּ תָ תַּ תָ תַּ תָ

7 בָּ תַּ שָׁ דָ רָ שָׁ דֶ שָׁ בֶּ תֶּ בָּ רַ

8 שָׁרַ בָּשָׁ דָבְ תֶּשָׁ רָתָ שָׁבָּ שֶׁ

9 שֵׁת   שָׂרֵת   שָׂשׂ   שָׁת   שַׁבָּת
  Seth   service   glad   put   Sabbath

10 דַת   בַּת   רַבַּת   רָתָת   בָּשָׂר
  religion   daughter   many (poetic form)   to tremble   meat

9

LETTERS YOU KNOW:

ת ֖ת שׁ שׂ ד ר ב בּ

T   T   S   SH   D   R   V   B

VOWELS YOU KNOW:

ָ   ַ   ֵ

AH   AH   AY

---

1. The LAHMED starts above the line so: ___ ל ___
    Write a row of 12 LAHMEDs beginning here _____

    _____

    _____

    Add the vowel AH   ַ   to the first 4 LAHMEDs.

    Add this vowel AH   ָ   to the next 4 LAHMEDs.

    Add the vowel AY   ֵ   to the last 4 LAHMEDs.

2. Now read aloud the row of letters and vowels you've just written.

3. Try it again to gain more speed.

4. Read these syllables:

		Now write their sounds.	
לֲ (2)	לָ (1)	_____ (2)	_____ (1)
לָ (2)	לֵ (1)	_____ (2)	_____ (1)
לֵ (2)	לַ (1)	_____ (2)	_____ (1)

5. Here is the MEM מ with the saying sound of _____.

6. Next to each MEM מ and vowel write its sound.

   This syllable מֵ reads _____

   This syllable מֶ reads _____

   This syllable מָ reads _____

7. Which sounds in this row read MAH MAH? Put a star over them.

   לְ לָ לֵ לֶ מֶ מֵ לֵ מָ מָ לָ לְ

8. Let's practice some reading aloud. We'll include all the letters you know.
   Do it slowly the first time. Then repeat it, increasing your speed with each reading.

   תֶ שַ רֵ רָ תָ שָ מֶ בָ לְ בֵ

   (If you had any difficulty remembering Hebrew letters or vowels, refer to the top of the
   page at the beginning of this Lesson.)

9. Now try speed-reading two syllables aloud.

   בֵּמֶ בַבֵ שָׁבֵ תַד תָּר לָב שָׁמֵ

10. You know how we write the word for heart, LAY-V. We use the LAHMED ל , the

    vowel AY •• and the VET ב , so: לֵב . Now you write it the

    way it is sometimes written: LAY-VAH-V. _____

11. Fill in the correct vowels to make this word read LAH-MAH-D. למד

12. And make this word read LAH-VAH-SH. לבש

13. This word מָר reads MAHR.

    You write the word SHAH-MAHR. _____

11

Can you find the first word in BAR MITZVAH below?
How about the first word in BAT MITZVAH?

1   בּ בּ ר ד שׂ שׁ ל מ תּ ת .. ָ ־

2   בְּ בַּ רָ דַ שָׁ שֶׁ לָ מֶ תֶּ תָּ

3   רַבּ שַׁבּ דָבּ בָּר לָמֶ מָשָׁ

בֶּר	שָׁר	שַׁר	מַר	תָּמָר
son	sings	leader	Mr.	date

4

שֵׁשׁ	שֵׁב	שֵׁת	לָתֶת	שָׁרֵת
six	sit!	Seth	to give	service

5

בַּת	דָת	שָׁת	רַבַּת	שַׁבָּת
daughter	religion	put	many	Sabbath

6

רַב	בָּד	שָׁב	שָׁשׂ	רֵשׁ
rabbi	linen	returned	glad	"R"

7

דָבָר	שָׁבַר	שָׁמַר	שַׁמָשׁ
thing	broke	guarded	attendant

8

לָבַשׁ	לֵבָב	בַּלֵּבָב	לָמַד
wore	heart	in the heart	studied

9

מָשָׁל	בָּרָד	דָּרַשׁ	דַּבֵּר
proverb	hail	explained	speak!

10

12

NEW VOWELS:

וֹ וֹ

OO   O

NEW LETTER:

ם

FINAL M

LETTERS YOU KNOW:

ל מ ת תּ שׂ שׁ ד ר בֿ בּ

L M T T S SH D R V B

VOWELS YOU KNOW:

אָ אַ אֵ

AH AH AY

---

1. Let's have a quiz to see how many letters you can identify. Next to each letter write its saying sound.

   f. _____ ל

   g. _____ ד

   h. _____ תּ

   i. _____ ר

   j. _____ שׁ

   a. _____ שׂ

   b. _____ מ

   c. _____ בּ

   d. _____ תּ

   e. _____ בֿ

   (Check your answers at the top of the page.)

2. This will be more difficult. We'll give you their names, you write the correct Hebrew letter next to each one. Ready?

   f. RAYSH _____

   g. TAHV _____

   h. SHEEN _____

   i. BET _____

   a. MEM _____

   b. LAHMED _____

   c. DAHLET _____

   d. SEEN _____

   e. VET _____

3. When we say that a letter is a FINAL LETTER you know that it is used only at the

   _____ of a word. This letter ◻ used only at the end of a word is

   _____ MEM.

4. After each syllable in this row, add the FINAL MEM

   ___ בְּ   ___ דָ   ___ תִ.   ___ שֶׁ   ___ לְ

5. Read the phrases you've just written. Then re-read them more speedily. Remember accuracy first, then speed.

6. Here are the two new vowels: O as in NO וֹ and OO as in FOOD וּ .
   Write the sounds under each of these letters combined with the vowel O

   מוֹ   לוֹ   שׁוֹ   תוֹ   דוֹ

   _____ _____ _____ _____ _____ ⟵

7. Now let's add the FINAL MEM and read these syllables:

   דוֹם תוֹם שׁוֹם לוֹם מוֹם ⟵

8. Practice reading aloud the vowel OO וּ now.

   מוּמוּ תוּתוּ לוּלוּ שׁוּשׁוּ ⟵

9. Read each of these words aloud carefully, then draw a circle around the one that reads SHAH-M.

   שָׁם שָׁם שָׁלֵם שֵׁם ⟵

10. This word דוֹר reads DOR.

    Add the vowels that will make this word read DOROT. ד ר ת

11. Remember this word? שָׁלוֹם

    It reads _____.

12. Write the Hebrew words for SHAH-BAHT   SHAH-LOM.

    _____ ⟵

14

Look for some Hebrew words here that are connected
with special Jewish holidays. Can you find them?

1   וֹ וּ וֹ וּ וֹ וָ וֹ וֹ ֵ ־ וֹ ־ ֵ וּ ָ

2   ל ם מ ם ל מ ם ל

3   לוּמֶ לָמֶ שׁוּם שָׁמֵ לוֹב לוֹב לָב

4   מָרוּ דָרוּ שָׁלוּ שֶׁל שָׁלֶ בַּל

5   בָּרוּ מַבּוּ תּוֹרְ לוֹם לֶם רוֹם

settlement	bitter herbs	flood	lulav
מוֹשָׁב	מָרוֹר	מַבּוּל	לוּלָב	6

studies	studied	wears	wore
לוֹמֵד	לָמַד	לוֹבֵשׁ	לָבַשׁ	7

there	puts	blood	high	high place	south	Mr.
שָׁם	שָׂם	דָם	רָם	מָרוֹם	דָרוֹם	מָר	8

Sabbath	greetings	whole	attendant	name
שַׁבָּת	שָׁלוֹם	שָׁלֵם	שַׁמָשׁ	שֵׁם	9

uncle	generation	clear	three	His Torah
דוֹד	דוֹר	בָּרוּר	שָׁלֹשׁ	תּוֹרָתוֹ	10

15

NEW LETTERS:

ן	ו	י
FINAL N	V	Y

LETTERS YOU KNOW:

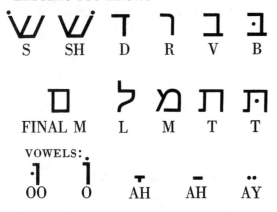

שׂ	שׁ	ד	ר	בּ	בּ
S	SH	D	R	V	B

ם	ל	מ	ת	תּ
FINAL M	L	M	T	T

VOWELS:

וּ	וֹ	ָ	ַ	ֵ
OO	O	AH	AH	AY

---

1. Here is the smallest letter in the Hebrew alphabet י . Its name is YUD and its

   saying sound is _____.

2. Add the correct vowel to each YUD י to complete the sound required.

י	י	י	י	י
_____	_____	_____	_____	_____
YAH	YOO	YAY	YAH	YO
   ←

3. Read over the sounds you've completed above.

   a. Now cover the English letters and read the syllables again. Check your answer to be sure you're reading it correctly.

   b. Try speed-reading the line this time.

4. Match these two columns.

YOO	( )		(1)	יֵ
YAH	( )		(2)	יַ
YO	( )		(3)	יוּ
YAY	( )		(4)	יוֹ

5. One of these words reads YOM as in YOM KIPPUR. Which one? ( )

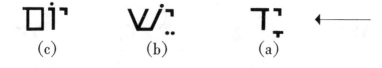

יוֹם	שֵׁם	דַת	
(c)	(b)	(a)	←

16

6. Even though VAHV ו and VET ב have the same saying sound you know that they are two different letters.

   Both ו and ב have the saying sound of _____ .

7. Under each syllable write its sound.

   בֻ   בָ   בוֹ   בוּ   בֹ

   _____ _____ _____ _____ _____

8. Next to each of these letters and vowels write the sound.

   This syllable   בָ   reads _____ .

   This syllable   בֵ   reads _____ .

   This syllable   בֹ   reads _____ .

   This syllable   בִי   reads _____ .

9.   ב   is called _____ and has the saying sound of _____ .

   ו   is called _____ and has the saying sound of _____ .

   ן   is called FINAL NUN and has the saying sound of _____ .

10. Because it is used only at the end of a word ן is called _____ _____ .

11. Combined with the BET בּ , the SHEEN שׁ , and the TAHV תּ , here are three words ending with the FINAL NUN.
    Under each one write its sound.

    תֵּן   שֵׁן   בֵּן

    _____ _____ _____

12. Using YUD, VAHV and FINAL NUN, write the Hebrew word for "Greek," YAH-VAH-N. (use this vowel ָ AH)

    _____   ←—

Sometimes people confuse the י , the ו , and the final ן . Be sure you don't.

1   יֹ יֹו יָ יֵ יַ יֵ יָ יֵּ ַ יֵ

2   רֵ וָ וו וו וַ וו וֵ רֵ

3   לון שׁון בָּן וָן שֵׁן שֵׁן שָׁן

4   לַיו לִי בָּיו בַּי דֵּי דַּי תַּי

5   יוֹמָ שָׁשׁ יָשׁ יוֹשׁ יָן יוֹתֵ יָר יוֹר

6   יוֹתֵר / יָרַשׁ (inherited) / יוֹרֵשׁ (heir) / יָרַד (went down) / יוֹרֵד (goes down)
more   inherited   heir   went down   goes down

7   בֵּית (house of)   בֵּין (between)   יֵשׁ (there is)   בַּיוֹם (on the day)   יוֹם (day)   יָם (sea)

8   וָו (hook)   תַּיָר (tourist)   יָשׁוּב (will return)   יָשַׁב (sat)   יוֹשֵׁב (sits)

9   מָלוֹן (hotel)   שֵׁן (tooth)   יָשֵׁן (sleeps)   יָשָׁר (straight, honest)   יָשָׁן (old)

10   יָד (hand)   לָשׁוֹן (language)   מוּבָן (meaning)   מַתָּן (gift)   דַּיָן (judge)

NEW VOWEL—SILENT: NEW LETTERS— SILENT:

: ע א

LETTERS YOU KNOW:

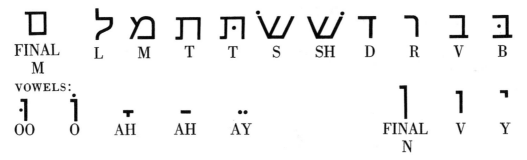

ם	ל	מ	ת	תּ	שׂ	שׁ	ד	ר	בּ	בּ
FINAL M	L	M	T	T	S	SH	D	R	V	B

VOWELS:

וּ	וֹ	ָ	ַ	ֵ		ן	ו	י
OO	O	AH	AH	AY		FINAL N	V	Y

---

1. AHLEF **א** and AHYIN **ע** are the two SILENT LETTERS.
   Write the letter called for.

   _____ _____ _____ _____ _____ _____ _____ ←

   AHLEF   AHLEF   AHYIN   AHLEF   AHYIN   AHYIN   AHLEF

2. We've written the letters this time. You add the correct vowels. Don't let the
   O and OO fool you.

   א ע ע א ע א א ע א ←

   OO   AH   AY   OO   AH   O   AH   O   AY

   (Check your answers at the top of the page.)

3. Read the sounds you've just completed in the row above. Is your speed improving?
   Cover the English sounds and read the row again.

4. Here are the **א** and **ע** combined with vowels plus the FINAL NUN **ן** or
   FINAL MEM **ם** . Fill in the sounds under each one.

   עֵן אֶם אוֹם אָן עַם ←

   _____ _____ _____ _____ _____

5. Now fill in these sounds.

   עַל עֵת אֶל אַת אוֹר עַד ←

   _____ _____ _____ _____ _____ _____

6. Remember what you learned about the vowel O? In most cases it is written this

way וֹ . Sometimes it appears only as a dot ׁ over a letter.

Can you read this word? רֹאשׁ

The saying sound of the first letter ר is _____ .

The vowel ׁ is _____ .

The saying sound of the next letter א is_____ .

The saying sound of the last letter שׁ is_____ .

The word רֹאשׁ reads _____ .

7. Now try this one: עוֹלָם

The saying sound of the first letter ע is _____ .

The vowel וֹ is_____ .

The saying sound of the next letter ל is _____ .

The next vowel ָ is_____ .

The saying sound of the last letter ם is _____ .

When you see the word עוֹלָם you read it _____ . It means "universe,"
or "world."

8. The silent vowel ְ SHVAH is written under a Hebrew letter.

It has _____ sound.

9. Write the SHVAH under each of these letters.

DAHLET   SHEEN   LAHMED   BET   VAHV

ד   שׁ   ל   בּ   ו

10. Practice reading the sounds you've just completed. Now cover the names above each
letter. Do you recognize the letters? Know what to do if you don't recognize each letter?

This time there are two reading drill sheets, with many words you'll find in prayers. See how many you recognize. Have you noticed how many numbers have been included? Do you remember how to say NINE, FOUR, THREE, SIX?

1   אַ   אָ   אֶ   אוֹ   אוֹ   אֶ   אֶ   אוֹ   אַ   אוּ

2   עַ   עָ   עֶ   עוֹ   עֶ   עוֹ   עָ   עֶ   עוֹ   עֶ   עוֹ

3   א   ע   ע   א   ע   א   ע   א   ע   א   ע

4   בְּ   דוּ   עַ   שׁוּ   תְּ   יוֹ   אֶ   לְ   עוּ

5   עַם   אֶם   לֹא   אֵין   עַל   אָב

6   אָבוּ   מָבוֹ   אָרוּ   אָד   אַבָּא

7   שָׁא   שֶׁא   עָמַ   אָמַ   אֲבָל

8   עוֹבֶ   מוֹעַ   אוֹמֶ   שׁוֹא   אֶשׁ

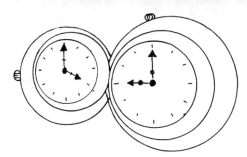

מָבוֹא introduction	אָדוֹן Mr., sir	אָרוֹן ark	אָבוֹת fathers	1
מַדוּעַ why	לָדַעַת to know	יָדַע knew	יוֹדֵעַ knows	2
שָׁאַל asked	שׁוֹאֵל asks	אָמַר said	אוֹמֵר says	3
לַעֲשׂוֹת to do	לַעֲבֹד to work	עָבַד worked	עוֹבֵד works	4
שָׂשׂוֹן rejoicing	לַעֲמֹד to stand	עָמַד stood	עוֹמֵד stands	5
שָׁבוּעוֹת weeks, Festival of Weeks	שָׁבוּעַ week	שְׁמַע hear!	שׁוֹמֵעַ hears	6
לְמַעַן for the sake of	מְאֹד very	לְעַמּוֹ to his people	עַמּוֹ his people	7
שָׁעוֹן clock	אַרְבַּע four	תֵּשַׁע nine	בְּתֵאָבוֹן good appetite!	8

22

NEW LETTERS:

גּ ן נ
G   N

LETTERS YOU KNOW:

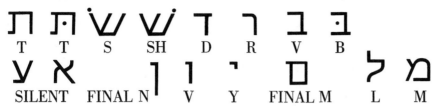

ת תּ שׂ שׁ ד ר בּ ב
T   T   S   SH D   R   V   B

ע א ן וּ ו י ם ל מ
SILENT FINAL N V Y FINAL M L M

VOWELS YOU KNOW:

שְׁ   וּ   וֹ   ָ   ַ   ֵ
SILENT OO   O   AH   AH   AY

---

1. The regular NUN used at the beginning or middle of a word is written **נ** .

   This letter **ן** used only at the end of a word is _____ _____

2. NUN is written _____ . GIMEL is written _____ .

3. Here is a row of NUNs and GIMELs. Under each letter write its saying sound.

   גּ נ נ גּ נ גּ נ גּ גּ ←

   _____ _____ _____ _____ _____ _____ _____ _____ _____

4. Now we'll add vowels to the **נ** and **גּ** . Under each syllable fill in its sound.

   נְגוּ גְ נֵ נוּ נוֹ גוֹ ←

   _____ _____ _____ _____

5. Practice reading the line above.

   a. Cover the English sounds and read the line again.
   b. Are you able to read it accurately as well as speedily?

6. Practice reading these sounds you know with the FINAL NUN **ן** added.

   נִן גִן נוּן נוֹן נָן גַן

7. Below are letters you know. We've given their names, you supply their saying sounds.

AHLEF **MEM** **TAHV** **SHEEN** **RAYSH** **YUD** **VAHV**

א   מ   תּ   שׁ   ר   י   ו

_____ _____ _____ _____ _____ _____ _____

8. Fill in the correct vowels to complete these sounds:

LAY **NOO** **B** **GO** **AH** **YO** **SHAY**

ל   נ   בְּ   גֹ   עַ   יִ   שׁ   ⟵

_____ _____ _____ _____ _____ _____ _____

9. The Hebrew ending   נוּ   on a word usually means "our." It is used very often. Let's practice reading it.

The word   אָנוּ   is read _____.

The word   בָּנוּ   is read _____.

The word   לָנוּ   is read _____.

10. Let's try a few more.

This syllable   מֵנוּ   is read _____.

This syllable   שִׁנוּ   is read _____.

This syllable   תֵנוּ   is read _____.

11. Here are three words. One of them reads AH-LAY-NOO. Which one? ( )

עָלֵינוּ   גָּדוֹל   גָּאַל   ⟵

(c)   (b)   (a)

12. And here are three more words. Which one reads MAH-GAY-N? ( )

נוֹרָא   מָגֵן   נָתַן

(c)   (b)   (a)

Here's another review lesson. Be sure you can read all the exercises with ease before you go on to Lesson 10. It really gets hard later on. Don't forget to turn to the second page of this reading drill!

1	נַ	נוּ	בָ	בֵ	בוּ	נַ	נֻ	בוּ	נֹ	נוּ
2	גַ	גוּ	גָ	גֵ	גוּ	גַ	גֻ	גֹ	גוּ	
3	ג	נ	ב	ג	נ	ב	ג	נ	ב	נ	ג	ב	נ
4	בֵ	רַ	וָ	לוֹ	אִ	תֶ	יַ	עוּ	שׁוֹ	מוּ
5	נוֹתֶ	נוֹשֵׁ	נוֹדֶ	נוֹא	נוֹגֶ					
6	גָדוּ	גוֹמֶ	גָמָ	תַּג	גוֹאֶ	אַגוֹ				
7	שָׁבֵ	גְבוּ	גָמָ	עֵבַ	גָדוּ	מְבַ				
8	בָּנוּ	דֶנוּ	יָנוּ	מָנוּ	עָלֵינוּ					

25

Here are more words and their meanings.

גּוֹי	גֵּר	גַּם	נֵר	גַּן	בְּנֵי	1
nation	stranger	also	candle	garden	children of	

אֲבוֹתֵינוּ	דּוֹרֵנוּ	רַגְלֵינוּ	לָנוּ	2
our fathers	our age / our generation	our feet	to us	

מְנַגֵּן	לְנַגֵּן	לָגוּר	גָּר	3
plays (an instrument)	to play (an instrument)	to live	lives	

גָּאוֹן	גַּדְּלוּ	גָּדַל	גָּדוֹל	4
genius; gaon — a rabbinic title	magnify!	grew, became big	great, big	

גְּמָרָא	מָגֵן	גּוֹאֵל	5
part of the Talmud	shield	redeemer	

אֲגוֹרוֹת	תַּרְנְגֹל	גָּמָל	6
Israeli coins	rooster	camel	

נָשָׂא	נוֹשֵׂא	נָדַד	נוֹדֵד	7
carried	carries	wandered	wanders	

גָּמַר	גּוֹמֵר	נָתַן	נוֹתֵן	8
finished	finishes	gave	gives	

NEW VOWEL:

∵

EH as in PET

NEW LETTERS:

ח ח

H   CH

LETTERS YOU KNOW:

ל מ תּ ת שׂ שׁ ד ר בּ בּ

L   M   T   T   S   SH   D   R   V   B

ג נ ע א ן וּ ו י ם

G   N   SILENT   FINAL N   V   Y   FINAL M

VOWELS:

׃ וֹ וּ ָ ַ ֵּ

SILENT   OO   O   AH   AH   AY

---

1. This vowel וּ is _____. This vowel ָ is _____.

   This vowel וֹ is _____. This vowel ַ is_____.

   This vowel ׃ is _____. This vowel ֵ is_____.

   The new vowel ∵ is _____ as in _____.

2. Practice reading these vowels.

   ׃ ∵ ָ ַ ∵ ֵ ׃ ∵ ָ וֹ ֵ וּ ַ ָ ←

3. Here are the two new letters.

   This ח is CHET; its saying sound is_____.

   This ה is HAY; its saying sound is_____.

4. The Hebrew sound that does *not* appear in the English alphabet is called

   _____. It is written so: _____.

5. This syllable ח reads_____.

   This syllable ה reads_____.

27

6. Under each syllable write its sound.

$\leftarrow$ חַ   חֶ   הוֹ   הוֹ   חֳ   חָ   חֲ

_____ _____ _____ _____ _____ _____ _____

7. Cover the English sounds you've just written and practice reading.
   a. Reading the CHET slows your speed a bit, doesn't it?
   b. Try the line again.

8. We'll add the RAYSH ר and the DAHLET ד to the new letters

   HAY ה and CHET ח.

   Complete each sound by filling in the correct vowel.

   $\leftarrow$ ח   ד   ח   ה   ר   ה

   _____ _____ _____ _____ _____ _____

   HEH   RAH   CHO   HAH   DOO   CHAY

9. Match these words with their correct sounds. Watch out these are tricky!

H-AY-M ( )	(1)	חַם
CH-AY-N ( )	(2)	חֵם
CH-AH-M ( )	(3)	חֵן

10. The Hebrew word for room is חֶדֶר.

    חֶדֶר is read _____.

11. At the end of a word the HAY ה is not sounded. When you see the word for the

    special Sabbath and holiday bread חַלָה you read it _____

    and you don't sound the ה at the end.

12. One of these words reads HAH-YAH. $\leftarrow$ חַג   חָדָשׁ   הָיָה

    This word reads HAH-YAH.

    _____

You'll recognize many words here that you've heard in song and in prayer. Now you can read them. And are you remembering all the numbers so far? Here are a few more.

ה ה ה ה ח ה ה ח ח ה ה   1

נ ג ג ג נ ג נ ג נ ג נ   2

א ע א ע ע ע א ע ע   3

ו ן ו י י ו ן י ו י ן ו   4

וּ וּ וּ וּ וּ וּ וּ וּ וּ וּ וּ וּ   5

  6

  7

הוֹ חוּ חַ הֶ הוּ חִ הֵ חַ הֶ ה חוּ חֻ   8

הֵי הָיוּ הַשָּׁ חָד חֹד חַמֵּ חֻם   9

אֶל עֶר אֶת אַח תַּח חַבֵּ חוֹשׁ   10

29

אַתָּה	אַתְּ	יַלְדָּה	יֶלֶד	חֲבֵרָה	חָבֵר	1
you (masc.)	you (fem.)	girl	boy	friend (fem.)	friend (masc.)

הַלְלוּיָה	הַלְלוּ	אֱלֹהֵינוּ	אֱלֹהֵי	2
praise ye the Lord!	praise!	our God	God of

חוֹשֶׁבֶת	חוֹשֵׁב	אוֹהֶבֶת	אוֹהֵב	3
thinks (fem.)	thinks (masc.)	likes (fem.)	likes (masc.)

תּוֹדָה	חַג	מָחָר	הַיּוֹם	תּוֹרָה	4
thank you	holiday	tomorrow	today	Torah

מַחְבֶּרֶת	חֶדֶר	חָדָשׁ	חֹדֶשׁ	5
notebook	room	new	month

הַגָּדָה	הַלֵּילוֹת	אֶתְרוֹג	6
narrative	the nights	etrog

הַשָּׁעָה	שֶׁבַע	חָמֵשׁ	אַחַת	אֶחָד	7
the time	seven	five	one (fem.)	one (masc.)

שֶׁמֶשׁ	לֶחֶם	גְּבֶרֶת	רֶגֶל	עֶרֶב	8
sun	bread	Mrs.	foot	evening

יָרֵחַ	שׁוֹלֵחַ	לוּחַ	שָׂמֵחַ	רוּחַ	9
moon	send	blackboard	happy	spirit, wind

אֵין חָדָשׁ תַּחַת הַשֶּׁמֶשׁ. 10

There is nothing new under the sun.(Proverb)

NEW LETTERS:

כַ   כ   כ
FINAL CHAHF   KAHF   CHAHF

LETTERS YOU KNOW:

ם   ל   מ   ת   תּ   שׂ   שׁ   ד   ר   ב   בּ
FINAL M   L   M   T   T   S   SH   D   R   V   B

ה   ח   ג   נ   עא   ן   ו   וֹ   י
H   CH   G   N   SILENT   FINAL N   V   Y

VOWELS:

ֱ   ְ   וּ   וֹ   ָ   ַ   ֵ
EH   SILENT   OO   O   AH   AH   AY

1. CHAHF כ and CHET ח have the same saying sound. This is the sound not found in the English alphabet.

   כ and ח have the saying sound of _____.

2. Add a dot to the CHAHF כ so: כּ and the letter becomes_____.

3. The saying sound of this letter כ is_____.

   The saying sound of this letter כּ is_____.

4. Here is a row of CHAHFs and KAHFs. Under each letter write its saying sound.

   כּ   כ   כ   כ   כּ   כ   כּ   כּ   כ ←

_____

5. Let's practice reading כ and כּ combined with vowels you know.

   כֹוכִו   כָּכָ   כֹוכִו   כֹו   כֶּ   כָ   כ   כֵּ ←

6. Here are the BET בּ and VET ב. Do you confuse them with כּ and כ? Let's find out. Fill in the saying sounds.

   בּ   ב   כּ   כּ   כ   ב   כּ   בּ

_____

7. Now try vowels combined with KAHF כּ CHAHF כ BET בּ and VET ב

   כֶּ   בֹו   כֹו   בַ   כֶּ   כָ   בֵ   כֵּ ←

_____

8. Can you read this word? כְּבוֹד We've added the DAHLET דָ and a

vowel to the כְּ and the בֹ .

Let's work it out—   כְּ is _____

בוֹ is _____

ד is _____

The word כְּבוֹד is read _____. It means "glory of."

9. Let's try another חָכָם This syllable חָ reads _____

כָ reads _____

This Final Letter ם reads _____

The word חָכָם means "wise man," "sage." חָכָם reads _____.

If you are able to read חָכָם you are indeed wise.

10. Here are the FINAL letters you've learned so far: ם = Final _____

ן = Final _____

and this letter ך is Final CHAHF

11. Just as ם and ן appear only at the end of a word, so too

ך FINAL _____.

12. Most times ך appears at the end of a word combined with the silent vowel

: SHVAH, so: ךְ The saying sound of this letter ךְ is _____.

13. Here is the word BLESSED or PRAISED that you have used many times בָּרוּךְ.

The word בָּרוּךְ reads _____.

14. This is a Blessing you've repeated from memory for a long time. Now read it.

בָּרוּךְ שֵׁם כְּבוֹד מַלְכוּתוֹ לְעוֹלָם וָעֶד

32

Some of these sounds will be a little rough on your throat, but you'll get used to them. Onward!

1 כַּ כּוֹ כֶּ כֵּ כּוּ כָּ כּוֹ כּוּ כֶּ כֵּ כַּ כֶּ

2 כַּ כּוֹ כֵּ כֶּ כּוֹ כָּ כּוּ כֵּ כֵּ כּוּ כֶּ כַּ כֶּ

3 דְּ דֵּ דִּ דֹ דּוּ דַּ דּוֹ דָּ דֶּ דֹ דּוּ דִּ דֹּ דֵּ דַּ

4 כ ח ה כ ח כ כ כ כ ה ח כ ה כ ח כ

5 כ ב כ כ ב כ ב כ ב כ כ ב כ ב כ ב כ

6 כְּבוֹ   כְּמוֹ   כָּחוּ   נָכוֹ   כּוּתוֹ

7 כּוֹב   כּוּת   כֵּת   כֹּה   בּוּכֶ

8 מוּכָ   מַלְכוּ   אֶשְׁכּוֹ   אוֹכֵ   עַכְשָׁ

9 רוּךְ   לֵךְ   מֶךְ   רָךְ   לֹךְ   שֶׁךְ

10 הֵךְ   בְּךָ   לֹךְ   שֶׁךְ   דֵּךְ   לוּךְ

11 וְאָהַבְתָּ לְרֵעֲךָ כָּמוֹךָ
Love your neighbor as yourself.

מַלְכוּתוֹ His kingdom	מַלְכוּת kingdom	מַלְכֵּנוּ our king	מֶלֶךְ king	**1**
כְּבוֹדוֹ His glory	כְּבוֹד glory	בָּרוּךְ blessed	בָּרְכוּ bless!	**2**
שֶׁבְּכָל that on all	וּבְכָל and with all	בְּכָל with all	כָּל all	**3**

כָּחֹל blue	כֹּחַ strength	כַּוָּנָה intention	כֹּהֵן *kohen*, priest	כֵּן yes	**4**
בֶּרֶךְ knee	דֶּרֶךְ road	כָּשֵׁר kosher	כֶּתֶר crown	כֹּתֶל wall	**5**

אוֹכֶלֶת she eats	אוֹכֵל he eats	כּוֹתֶבֶת she writes	כּוֹתֵב he writes	**6**
כְּמוֹ like, as	כַּמָה how many?	כְּבָר already	עַכְשָׁו now	**7**

חֹשֶׁךְ darkness	אֶשְׁכּוֹל bunch of grapes	כֶּלֶב dog	כַּדּוּר ball	כּוֹבַע hat	**8**

יֵשׁ לָךְ you have (fem.)	יֵשׁ לְךָ you have (masc.)	נָכוֹן correct	חָכָם wise	**9**

מַה שְׁלוֹמֵךְ? How are you? (fem.)	מַה שְׁלוֹמְךָ? How are you? (masc.)	**10**
	מַה שְׁמֵךְ? What's your name? (fem.)	**11**

34

NEW VOWELS:

IH   EE

LETTERS YOU KNOW:

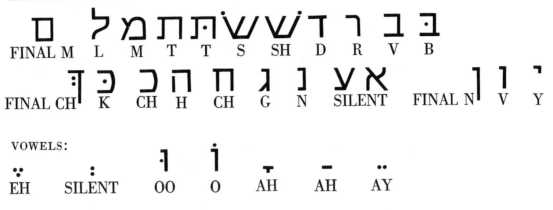

ם ל מ תּ ת שׁ ד ר ב בּ
FINAL M   L   M   T   T   S   SH   D   R   V   B

ךְ כּ כ הּ ח ג נ א ן ו וּ י
FINAL CH   K   CH   H   CH   G   N   SILENT   FINAL N   V   Y

VOWELS:

ֶ   ְ   וּ   וֹ   ָ   ַ   ֵ
EH   SILENT   OO   O   AH   AH   AY

Let's stop for another quiz to catch up on all you've learned so far.

1. Here are two rows of look-alike letters. First look at the letter in Row A. Then add a dot to each letter in Row B and write its name in the space provided.

ROW B			ROW A
_____ ב		VET	ב
_____ כ		CHAHF	כ
_____ ת		TAHV	ת

2. These are letters often confused for one another. You fill in the missing names.

_____ ד		RAYSH	ר
_____ נ		GIMEL	ג
_____ ח		CHET	ח
_____ ר		VAHV	ו

3. Here are pairs of letters with the same saying sound. Write the correct saying sounds.

a. _____ ח כ

b. _____ א ע

c. _____ תּ ת

d. _____ בּ ו

4. Each of these is a FINAL letter. Fill in the saying sounds.

ן ךָ ם

_____ _____ _____

5. Here again are the FINAL letters. Each one has a regular letter with the same name. Next to each FINAL letter, write the regular letter.

REGULAR		FINAL
_____	MEM	ם
_____	CHAHF	ךָ
_____	NUN	ן

6. We'll give you the vowel *sounds*. You fill in the vowels.

AH (2) _____   OO _____

O _____   IH _____

AY _____   EH _____

SILENT _____

7. You know that one dot . is the vowel IH as in TICK. How do you read one dot

followed by the YUD so: ִ ִי . is read _____ .

8. Here are letters you know. Some are combined with the vowel ◦ others with the vowel ⟨ ⟩ . Under each, write its sound.

כְּי   כֵּ   כָ   לִי   לְ   מִי   מְ   מָ

_____ _____ _____ _____ _____ _____ _____ _____

9. The YUD ◦ is used in other ways.

When ◦ follows ◦ the sound is AH EE (I) ◦

When ◦ follows ◦ the sound is AH EE (I) ◦

This word אֲדֹנָי reads _____ .

This word שַׁדַּי reads _____ .

10. This is one way to write the name by which God is known ◦ .

Here is another אֲדֹנָי . Both אֲדֹנָי and יְיָ mean _____ .

Though אֲדֹנָי and יְיָ are written differently, they are always read as

_____ . This too אֲדֹנָי is read as _____ .

11. Have you remembered that sometimes the ◦ is read as Y?

Under each syllable fill in its sound, and don't let the ◦ trick you.

יִ   תָי   הִי   יְ   כְּ   יוֹ   יֶ

_____ _____ _____ _____ _____ _____

12. This is the Hebrew word for Israel יִשְׂרָאֵל .

The word יִשְׂרָאֵל is read _____ .

13. Here's a prayer you've known by heart for a long time. It was probably the first one you memorized. Now you can read it.

שְׁמַע יִשְׂרָאֵל יְיָ אֱלֹהֵינוּ יְיָ אֶחָד

37

Here are the numbers 1 through 12 to help you tell time.

1	אַחַת (1)	שְׁתַּיִם (2)	שָׁלֹשׁ (3)	אַרְבַּע (4)
2	חָמֵשׁ (5)	שֵׁשׁ (6)	שֶׁבַע (7)	שְׁמֹנֶה (8)
3	תֵּשַׁע (9)	עֶשֶׂר (10)	אַחַת עֶשְׂרֵה (11)	רֶבַע a fourth a quarter
4	שְׁתֵּים עֶשְׂרֵה (12)	שָׁעָה time, hour	וְ... and	מַה הַשָּׁעָה? What time is it?

Using the masculine verb יָכוֹל and the feminine יְכוֹלָה (can, able) with the following infinitives, endless sentences can be formed.

5	לִלְמֹד to study	לִשְׁמֹעַ to hear	לִשְׁלֹחַ to send	לָשִׁיר to sing
6	לְחַכּוֹת to wait	לִרְאוֹת to see	לִכְתֹּב to write	לְהַכִּיר to know to be acquainted
7	לְדַבֵּר to speak	לַעֲשׂוֹת to do	לָלֶכֶת to go, to walk	לְהַתְחִיל to begin
8	עִבְרִית Hebrew	אַנְגְּלִית English	אֲנִי I	בַּיִת house	הַבַּיְתָה homeward

9 אֲנִי יָכוֹל לִכְתֹּב וּלְדַבֵּר עִבְרִית.

I can write and speak Hebrew.

THE SH'MA BLESSING

Hear, O Israel:
The Lord is our God, the Lord is One.

שְׁמַע יִשְׂרָאֵל יְיָ אֱלֹהֵינוּ יְיָ אֶחָד.   1

A RESPONSE AND A BLESSING

Blessed be His name whose glorious
kingdom is forever and ever.

בָּרוּךְ שֵׁם כְּבוֹד מַלְכוּתוֹ לְעוֹלָם וָעֶד.   2

BLESSINGS BEFORE READING THE TORAH

Bless the Lord, who is blessed!

בָּרְכוּ אֶת יְיָ הַמְבֹרָךְ.   3

Blessed be the Lord who is blessed
for ever and ever.

בָּרוּךְ יְיָ הַמְבֹרָךְ לְעוֹלָם וָעֶד.   4

Blessed are You, Lord,

בָּרוּךְ אַתָּה יְיָ   5

our God, King of the universe,

אֱלֹהֵינוּ מֶלֶךְ הָעוֹלָם   6

who chose us

אֲשֶׁר בָּחַר בָּנוּ   7

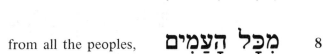

from all the peoples,

מִכָּל הָעַמִּים   8

and gave us His Torah.

וְנָתַן לָנוּ אֶת תּוֹרָתוֹ   9

Blessed are You, Lord, who gives the Torah.

בָּרוּךְ אַתָּה יְיָ נוֹתֵן הַתּוֹרָה.   10

39

Now you can read the **שְׁמַע**, sing
אֵין כֵּאלֹהֵינוּ, and count from
1 through 12. Good for you!

אֱלֹהֵי	אֲדוֹנָי	מֶלֶךְ	מוֹשִׁיעַ
God of	Lord	king	savior

אֱלֹהֵינוּ	אֲדוֹנֵינוּ	מַלְכֵּנוּ	מוֹשִׁיעֵנוּ
our God	our Lord	our King	our Savior

אֵין	מִי	נוֹדֶה	בָּרוּךְ	אַתָּה הוּא
none	who	we will give thanks	blessed	You are He

1   אֵין כֵּאלֹהֵינוּ   אֵין כַּאדוֹנֵינוּ

2   אֵין כְּמַלְכֵּנוּ   אֵין כְּמוֹשִׁיעֵנוּ

3   מִי כֵאלֹהֵינוּ   מִי כַאדוֹנֵינוּ

4   מִי כְמַלְכֵּנוּ   מִי כְמוֹשִׁיעֵנוּ

5   נוֹדֶה לֵאלֹהֵינוּ   נוֹדֶה לַאדוֹנֵינוּ

6   נוֹדֶה לְמַלְכֵּנוּ   נוֹדֶה לְמוֹשִׁיעֵנוּ

7   בָּרוּךְ אֱלֹהֵינוּ   בָּרוּךְ אֲדוֹנֵינוּ

8   בָּרוּךְ מַלְכֵּנוּ   בָּרוּךְ מוֹשִׁיעֵנוּ

9   אַתָּה הוּא אֱלֹהֵינוּ   אַתָּה הוּא אֲדוֹנֵינוּ

10   אַתָּה הוּא מַלְכֵּנוּ   אַתָּה הוּא מוֹשִׁיעֵנוּ

40

NEW VOWEL: **NEW LETTERS:**

◌ֻ   פ   פּ

U as in PUT   P   F

LETTERS YOU KNOW:

ם ל מ ת תּ שׂ שׁ ד ר ב בּ

FINAL M — L — M — T — T — S — SH — D — R — V — B

ך כ כּ ח ה חַ ג נ אָ ן ו וּ ִי

FINAL CH — K — CH — H — CH — G — N — SILENT — FINAL N — V — Y

VOWELS:

ִי   ִ   ֵ   ְ   וּ   וֹ   ָ   ַ   ֵ

EE — IH — EH — SILENT — OO — O — AH — AH — AY

---

1. FAY is written פ. It has *no* dot in the middle. Its saying sound is _____.

2. Match these columns   F ( )   (1) פֵ

   FAY ( )   (2) פוֹ

   FO ( )   (3) פְ

3. Here is a row of FAYs. Each פ is combined with a vowel you know. Write the complete sounds under each syllable.

   פִי   פֵ   פָ   פִ   פוֹ   פַ   פֵ

   _____ _____ _____ _____ _____ _____ _____

4. PAY is written פּ. It has a dot in the middle. Its saying sound is _____.

5. Under each letter write its saying sound.

   פ   פ   פ   פּ   פ   פּ   פ   פּ

   _____ _____ _____ _____ _____ _____ _____ _____

6. Read aloud these sounds, combining vowels you know with the פ and פּ.

   פָ   פוֹ   פַ   פֵ   פוֹ   פֵ   פֵ   פִ

   Now try reading the line a little faster.

7. We'll add more letters to this row. Fill in the sounds under each one, and

remember what you learned about רִ. EE.

רִ֫   כָ   בוּ   פִּי   פֵּ   כָ   בַ

_____ _____ _____ _____ _____ _____ _____

8. Here's a word you've heard many times. פֶּֽרֶךְ

Let's sound it out פֶּ is _____

רֶךְ is _____

The word פֶּֽרֶךְ is read _____

9. Can you read this word חֻמָשׁ It means "Five Books of Moses."

Work it out here: חֻ is read _____

מָ is read _____

שׁ is read _____

The word חֻמָשׁ is read _____ .

10. The vowel IH ִ has _____ dot;

AY ֵ has _____ dots;

The new vowel U ֻ has _____ dots.

11. Now you know two vowels consisting of three dots.

This vowel ֵ is _____ as in _____ .

This vowel ֻ is _____ as in _____ .

12. You also know two vowels consisting of two dots.

This vowel ֵ is _____ as in _____ .

This vowel ִ is called _____ and it is _____ .

13. Here are ALL the vowels you have learned. Under each write its sound.

רִ֫   וֹ   ְ   וֹ   ֻ   ֵ   ִ   ֵ   ־   ָ

_____ _____ _____ _____ _____ _____ _____ _____ _____ _____

By this time you should be able to write very simple sentences with all the words you've learned. Have you tried it?

1 פ פ פ פ פ פ פ פ פ פ פ פ פ פ

2 יְ   יְ   יֶ   ־   ֶ   ֱ   ֹ   ־   ֱ   יְ   ֶ   ֳ   יֶ   ֶ

3	שׁוֹפָר shofar	פְּרִי fruit	פֹּה here	עִפָּרוֹן pencil
4	פּוּרִים Purim	חֲנֻכָּה Chanukah	חֻמָּשׁ the Five Books of Moses	פָּרָשָׁה chapter, portion
5	יָפֶה nice (masc.)	יָפָה nice (fem.)	רוֹפֵא doctor	חָפְשִׁי free
6	אֵיפֹה where is?	אֶפְשָׁר maybe	אֲפִילוּ even	לִפְעָמִים sometimes
7	כִּפָּה skull cap	פֶּה mouth	פָּנִים face	אֲרֻחָה meal
8	מִשְׁפָּחָה family	תְּפִלָּה prayer	פּוֹתֵחַ opens	לַיְלָה night

BLESSING OVER WINE

9 בָּרוּךְ אַתָּה יְיָ אֱלֹהֵינוּ מֶלֶךְ הָעוֹלָם

Blessed are You, Lord, our God, King of the universe

10 בּוֹרֵא פְּרִי הַגָּפֶן.

who creates the fruit of the vine.

43

LETTERS YOU KNOW:

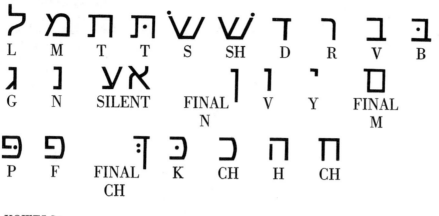

ל מ תּ ת שׂ שׁ ד ר ב בּ
L   M   T   T   S   SH D   R   V   B

גּ נ ע א ן ו י ם
G   N SILENT FINAL V   Y FINAL
             N   M

פּ פ ךּ ךּ כ ה ח
P   F FINAL K   CH H   CH
       CH

VOWELS:

ֻ ִי ִ ֵ ְ ּ וּ וֹ ָ ַ ֵ
U EE IH EH SILENT OO O AH AH AY

---

1. Here is the letter ט TET, sometimes confused with the MEM מ.

   The saying sound of ט is _____.

   The saying sound of מ is _____.

2. Do you mistake ט for מ ? Let's find out. Under each letter fill in its saying sound.

   מ   ט   מ   ט   ט   ט   מ   ט

   ___ ___ ___ ___ ___ ___ ___ ___

3. We've combined MEM מ and TET ט with vowels. Write their sounds under each.

   טֶ   מִי   טוֹ   מַ   טְ   טָ

   ___ ___ ___ ___ ___ ___

4. Read over the sounds you've just written above. Sure they're correct? Cover them now
   and practice reading the Hebrew syllables. Is your speed improving?

5. To complete each syllable in this row, you supply the correct vowel.

   MEH   TAH   MU   TOO   MIH   TAY   MO   TAH   MAH
   מ   ט   מ   ט   מ   ט   ט   ת   מ

   ___ ___ ___ ___ ___ ___ ___ ___ ___

6. Try speed-reading the row you've just finished. Cover the English sounds.

7. Here are the LAHMED ל , the TAHV ת , and the VET ב .
   We'll combine them with ט and מ for practice reading. Ready?

טַלִי תָב מָבוּ לַמֵ טַת לְבָב

8. The Hebrew word for "good" is טוֹב . Were you able to read טוֹב ?

   The word טוֹב reads _____

9. Here's another Hebrew word טַלִית . It means prayer shawl. Let's work it out.

   טַ reads _____

   לִי reads _____

   ת reads _____

   The word טַלִית reads _____.

10. This is the KOOF ק . This is the KAHF כ .

    Both have the saying sound of _____.

11. The Blessing recited over wine begins the KIH-DOO-SH. To complete the word
    KIH-DOO-SH, you fill in the vowels.

    קדושׁ

12. These are the last two words of the first Blessing in the קִדּוּשׁ

    פְּרִי הַגֶּפֶן

    They read _____ _____.

13. Can you read the entire Blessing?

    בָּרוּךְ אַתָּה יְיָ אֱלֹהֵינוּ מֶלֶךְ הָעוֹלָם
    בּוֹרֵא פְּרִי הַגָּפֶן .

How often have you heard your teacher say
Now you can read it. Very good!

1   טַ טוֹ טוּ טֶ טָ טְ קוֹ קַ קֶ קָ קֻ קְ

2   ט מ ט ט מ ט ט מ ט ט מ ט

3   ק כ ק כ ק כ ק כ ק כ ק כ ק

לַיְלָה טוֹב	עֶרֶב טוֹב	בֹּקֶר טוֹב	טוֹב
good night	good evening	good morning	good

4

טֵבֵת	טוּ בִּשְׁבָט	שְׁבָט	יוֹם טוֹב
Hebrew month	15th of Shevat	Hebrew month	holiday

5

מְקַדֵּשׁ	קִדְּשָׁנוּ	קֹדֶשׁ	קִדּוּשׁ	קָדוֹשׁ
sanctifies	sanctified us	holiness	sanctification	holy

6

קוֹרֵאת	קוֹרֵא	לְהַדְלִיק	טַלִּית
reads (fem.)	reads (masc.)	to kindle	prayer shawl

7

לִקְרֹא	אֲפִקוֹמָן	יְרָקוֹת	בְּבַקָשָׁה
to read	Afikomen, piece of mahtsah eaten after Seder meal	vegetables	please

8

קַל	נְקֻדוֹת	מִשְׁפָּט	קָפֶה	הַקָפוֹת
easy	vowels	judgment	coffee	processions

9

יַעֲקֹב	נָטַע	קֶרֶן	קְטַנָּה	קָטָן
Jacob	planted (masc.)	fund, horn	little (fem.)	little (masc.)

10

46

BLESSINGS AFTER READING THE TORAH

Blessed are You, Lord,	בָּרוּךְ אַתָּה יְיָ	1
our God, King of the universe,	אֱלֹהֵינוּ מֶלֶךְ הָעוֹלָם	2
who has given us the Torah of truth	אֲשֶׁר נָתַן לָנוּ תּוֹרַת אֱמֶת	3
and has implanted within us eternal life.	וְחַיֵּי עוֹלָם נָטַע בְּתוֹכֵנוּ.	4
Blessed are You, Lord,	בָּרוּךְ אַתָּה יְיָ	5
who gives the Torah.	נוֹתֵן הַתּוֹרָה.	6

SONGS BASED ON BIBLICAL VERSES

Behold how good and how pleasant it is	הִנֵּה מַה טּוֹב וּמַה נָּעִים	7
for brothers to dwell together as one. (Psalm 133)	שֶׁבֶת אַחִים גַּם יָחַד	
Nation shall not lift up sword against nation.	לֹא יִשָּׂא גוֹי אֶל גוֹי חֶרֶב	8
They shall not learn war anymore. (Isaiah 2:4; Micah 4:3)	לֹא יִלְמְדוּ עוֹד מִלְחָמָה	
How goodly are your tents, Jacob,	מַה טּוֹבוּ אֹהָלֶיךָ יַעֲקֹב	9
Your tabernacles, Israel. (Numbers 24:5)	מִשְׁכְּנֹתֶיךָ יִשְׂרָאֵל	

NEW LETTERS:

ז	ץ	צ
Z	FINAL TS	TS

LETTERS YOU KNOW:

ל	מ	ת	תּ	שׂ	שׁ	ד	ר	ב	בּ
L	M	T	T	S	SH	D	R	V	B

ג	נ	ע אּ	ן	ו	י	ם
G	N	SILENT	FINAL N	V	Y	FINAL M

ט	ק	פּ	פ	ךּ	כּ	כ	ה	ח
T	K	P	F	FINAL CH	K	CH	H	CH

VOWELS:

ֻ	ִי	ִ	ֵ	ְ	וּ	וֹ	ָ	ַ	ֵ
U	EE	IH	EH	SILENT	OO	O	AH	AH	AY

---

1. Here's the new letter with the unusual sound צ . It is called TSAHDEE.

   Its saying sound is _____ as in _____ .

2. The TSAHDEE צ is the Hebrew letter found in the word MATSOT. Put a circle around the TSAHDEE in the Hebrew word מַצּוֹת

3. The צ is found too, in the word MITSVAH מִצְוָה

   The name of this letter צ is _____ and its saying sound is _____ .

4. Do you recognize this well-known phrase? בַּר מִצְוָה

   The phrase בַּר מִצְוָה reads _____ _____ .

5. How about this phrase, recognize it? בַּת מִצְוָה

   The phrase בַּת מִצְוָה reads _____ _____ .

6. Sometimes the TSAHDEE **צ** is mistaken for the silent letter AHYIN: **ע**
   Do you make that mistake? Under each letter in this row write its saying sound.

   ע   **צ**   **ע**   **צ**   **ע**   **צ**   **צ**

   _____ _____ _____ _____ _____ _____ _____

7. Add the correct vowels to complete these syllables.

AY	TSU	TSEE	AH	OO	TSO	TSAY	TSAH
ע	**צ**	**צִי**	**ע**	**ע**	**צ**	**צ**	**צ**

   _____ _____ _____ _____ _____ _____ _____ _____

8. Now practice speed-reading the line above. Remember accuracy is most important.

9. The Blessing recited over bread is called **הַמוֹצִיא**.

   Can you read **הַמוֹצִיא** ?   Let's work it out.

   הַ reads _____

   מוֹ reads _____

   צִיא reads _____

   The word **הַמוֹצִיא** reads _____

10. Here is the FINAL TSAHDEE **ץ** . It appears only at the _____ of a word.

11. Can you read this word? It means land. **אֶרֶץ**

    The word **אֶרֶץ** reads _____.

    LAND OF ISRAEL is written: **אֶרֶץ יִשְׂרָאֵל**

    It reads _____ _____

12. Sometimes the ZAHYIN **ז** is mistaken for the VAHV **ו** Be on your guard.
    Under each of these syllables write their sounds.

    זֻ   **זָ**   **זְ**   **וֹז**   **ז**   **זֵ**   **זִ**

    _____ _____ _____ _____ _____ _____ _____

Here are some letters that are easily confused. Are you sure you can read each one correctly? Don't be fooled.

1	ז	ז	צ	ץ	ז	צ	ץ	ז	צ	צ	ז	צ	ץ

2	ע	צ	צ	ע	צ	צ	ע	צ	צ	ע	צ

מַצָה זו

3	אֶרֶץ	צִיוֹן	אַרְצוֹת הַבְּרִית
	land	Zion	United States

4	מַזָל	מָזוֹן	מְצֻיָן	מַצָה	מַצוֹת
	luck	food	excellent	unleavened bread (sing.)	(plural)

5	מִצְוָה	מִצְוֹת	מִצְוֹתָיו	בְּמִצְוֹתָיו
	commandment	commandments	His commandments	by His commandments

6	זֶה	זֹאת	זְמַן	בַּזְמַן הַזֶה
	this (masc.)	this (fem.)	time, season	at this time

7	זְמִירוֹת	מְזוּזָה	זָהָב	בֵּיצָה	זֵכֶר
	hymns, songs	mezuzah	gold	egg	in remembrance

8	זִכָּרוֹן	רוֹצֶה	רוֹצָה	צוֹחֵק	יִצְחָק
	memorial, reminder	want, wish (masc.)	want, wish (fem.)	laughs (masc.)	Isaac

9	עֵץ	עֵצִים	זוּזִים	יוֹם הָעַצְמָאוּת
	tree	trees	silver coins	Independence Day

10	צוּר	הַמוֹצִיא	הוֹצִיאָנוּ	מִמִצְרַיִם
	rock, God	who brings forth	brought us out	from Egypt

50

BLESSING OVER SABBATH LIGHTS

Blessed are You, Lord,	בָּרוּךְ אַתָּה יְיָ	1
our God, King of the universe	אֱלֹהֵינוּ מֶלֶךְ הָעוֹלָם	2
who has sanctified us	אֲשֶׁר קִדְּשָׁנוּ	3
by His commandments	בְּמִצְוֹתָיו	4
and commanded us	וְצִוָּנוּ	5
to kindle	לְהַדְלִיק	6
the Sabbath light.	נֵר שֶׁל שַׁבָּת.	7

BLESSING OVER WINE

Blessed are You, Lord,	בָּרוּךְ אַתָּה יְהוָה	1
our God, King of the universe,	אֱלֹהֵינוּ מֶלֶךְ הָעוֹלָם	2
who creates the fruit of the vine.	בּוֹרֵא פְּרִי הַגָּפֶן.	3

BLESSING OVER BREAD

Blessed are You, Lord,	בָּרוּךְ אַתָּה יְהוָה	1
our God, King of the universe	אֱלֹהֵינוּ מֶלֶךְ הָעוֹלָם	2
who brings forth bread from the earth.	הַמּוֹצִיא לֶחֶם מִן הָאָרֶץ.	3

BLESSING ON SPECIAL OCCASIONS

Blessed are You, Lord,	בָּרוּךְ אַתָּה יְיָ	1
our God, King of the universe	אֱלֹהֵינוּ מֶלֶךְ הָעוֹלָם	2
who has given us life	שֶׁהֶחֱיָנוּ	3
and sustained us	וְקִיְּמָנוּ	4
and brought us	וְהִגִּיעָנוּ	5
to this season.	לַזְּמַן הַזֶּה.	6

Blessed are You, Lord,	בָּרוּךְ אַתָּה יְיָ	1
our God, King of the universe	אֱלֹהֵינוּ מֶלֶךְ הָעוֹלָם	2
who made us holy by His commandments	אֲשֶׁר קִדְּשָׁנוּ בְּמִצְוֹתָיו	3
and favored us	וְרָצָה בָנוּ	4
and gave us as an inheritance His holy Sabbath in love and in favor,	וְשַׁבַּת קָדְשׁוֹ בְּאַהֲבָה וּבְרָצוֹן הִנְחִילָנוּ	5
a reminder of the works of Creation.	זִכָּרוֹן לְמַעֲשֵׂה בְרֵאשִׁית.	6
For it is a first day among the festivals of holiness,	כִּי הוּא יוֹם תְּחִלָּה לְמִקְרָאֵי קֹדֶשׁ	7
a reminder of the Exodus from Egypt.	זֵכֶר לִיצִיאַת מִצְרָיִם.	8
For You have chosen us	כִּי בָנוּ בָחַרְתָּ	9
and have made us holy among all the peoples,	וְאוֹתָנוּ קִדַּשְׁתָּ מִכָּל הָעַמִּים	10
and have given us as an inheritance Your holy Sabbath in love and in favor.	וְשַׁבַּת קָדְשְׁךָ בְּאַהֲבָה וּבְרָצוֹן הִנְחַלְתָּנוּ.	11
Blessed are You, Lord,	בָּרוּךְ אַתָּה יְיָ	12
who makes the Sabbath holy.	מְקַדֵּשׁ הַשַּׁבָּת.	13
Blessed are you, Lord,	בָּרוּךְ אַתָּה יְיָ	14
our God, King of the universe	אֱלֹהֵינוּ מֶלֶךְ הָעוֹלָם	15
who creates the fruit of the vine.	בּוֹרֵא פְּרִי הַגָּפֶן.	16

1   בָּרוּךְ אַתָּה יְיָ אֱלֹהֵינוּ מֶלֶךְ הָעוֹלָם   Blessed are You, Lord, our God,
King of the universe

2   אֲשֶׁר בָּחַר בִּנְבִיאִים טוֹבִים   who has chosen good prophets

3   וְרָצָה בְדִבְרֵיהֶם הַנֶּאֱמָרִים בֶּאֱמֶת.   and has found delight in their
words spoken in truth.

4   בָּרוּךְ אַתָּה יְיָ הַבּוֹחֵר בַּתּוֹרָה   Blessed are You, Lord, who has chosen the Torah

5   וּבְמֹשֶׁה עַבְדּוֹ וּבְיִשְׂרָאֵל עַמּוֹ   and Moses Your servant and Israel Your people

6   וּבִנְבִיאֵי הָאֱמֶת וָצֶדֶק.   and Your prophets of truth and righteousness.

FINAL F ף   ט S

LETTERS YOU KNOW:

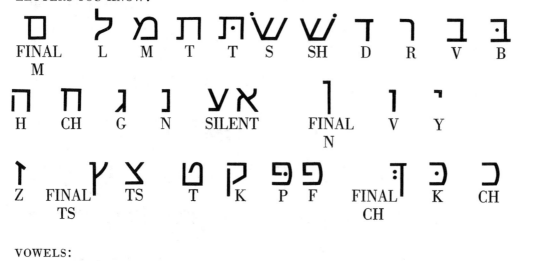

ם   ל   מ   ת   ת   שׂ   שׁ   ד   ר   ב   בּ
FINAL M   L   M   T   T   S   SH   D   R   V   B

ה   ח   ג   נ   אֲ   ן   ו   י
H   CH   G   N   SILENT   FINAL N   V   Y

ז   ץ   צ   ט   ק   פ   פּ   ךְ   כּ   כ
Z   FINAL TS   TS   T   K   P   F   FINAL CH   K   CH

VOWELS:

ֻ   ִי   ִ   ֶ   ְ   וּ   וֹ   ָ   ־   ֵ
U   EE   IH   EH   SILENT   OO   O   AH   AH   AY

---

1. We'll begin this lesson by reviewing the Hebrew letters in the order in which they appear in the Hebrew alphabet.
    You fill in the letter called for, under these first *seven* names.

    ZAHYIN   VAHV   HAY   DAHLET   GIMEL   BET   AHLEF

    _____ _____ _____ _____ _____ _____ _____   ←

2: Check with the letters at the top of the page to be certain you've written the letters correctly.

    Now cover the names and read aloud the names of the letters you've written.

    Try it again checking your answer with the name over each letter.

    Now without looking call out the letters beginning with AHLEF and ending with ZAHYIN.

    Did you get them all? GOOD!

3. Here are the next *seven* letters. Again write the Hebrew letter under each name.

   NUN   MEM   LAHMED   KAHF   YUD   TET   CHET

   ←————

   _____ _____ _____ _____ _____ _____ _____

4. Once again check with the letters at the top of the page.

   Review these letters now in the same way that you did with the first seven.

   Can you do it without looking, beginning with CHET and ending with NUN?

   Now try the 14 letters, beginning with AHLEF and ending with NUN.

5. The remaining *eight* letters beginning with the new letter SAHMECH complete the
   Hebrew alphabet.

   TAHV   SHEEN   RAYSH   KOOF   TSAHDEE   PAY   AHYIN   SAHMECH

   _____ _____ _____ _____ _____ _____ _____ _____

6. Do once again what you did with the first 14 letters.

   Memorize all 22 letters. Know them by heart!

   Ready to test yourself? Take a final look at all the letters.

   Now in its proper order beginning with א‎ and ending with ת‎ write each letter.

   _____ _____ _____ _____ _____ _____ _____ _____ _____
     (9)   (8)   (7)   (6)   (5)   (4)   (3)   (2)   (1)

   _____ _____ _____ _____ _____ _____ _____ _____ _____
    (18)   (17)   (16)   (15)   (14)   (13)   (12)   (11)   (10)

                                        _____ _____ _____ _____
                                         (22)   (21)   (20)   (19)

7. This time, in the same order, write the saying sounds for each of the 22 letters.

   _____ _____ _____ _____ _____ _____ _____ _____ _____
     (9)   (8)   (7)   (6)   (5)   (4)   (3)   (2)   (1)

   _____ _____ _____ _____ _____ _____ _____ _____ _____
    (18)   (17)   (16)   (15)   (14)   (13)   (12)   (11)   (10)

                                        _____ _____ _____ _____
                                         (22)   (21)   (20)   (19)

8. You noticed that only 22 letters were included in the Hebrew alphabet. Let's discover why. In each of these pairs of letters below the DOT changes the saying sound, but the outlines of both letters are the same, therefore only *one* is used in the alphabet.

   Fill in the name of the letter not used in the alphabet; we'll write the other.

   _____ בֿ   BET   בּ

   _____ כֿ   KAHF   כּ

   _____ פֿ   PAY   פּ

   _____ שׂ   SHEEN   שׁ

9. Here now is a review of the FINAL LETTERS including the FINAL FAY.
   Next to each FINAL LETTER write its saying sound.

   FINAL _____ ף   FINAL _____ ן   FINAL _____ ם ←

   FINAL _____ ץ   FINAL _____ ך

10. Here are the regular letters of the FINAL LETTERS we've just reviewed.
    Fill in their saying sounds.

    _____ נ   _____ צ   _____ מ   _____ כ ←

    _____ פ

11. Now write the regular Hebrew letters next to their FINAL outlines.

    ___ ץ   ___ ן   ___ ם   ___ ף   ___ ך ←

12. How well have you learned the vowels? Let's find out.
    Here are all the sounds. You fill in the vowels.

    ___ ___ ___ ___ ___ ___ ___ ___ ___ ___ ←
    SILENT   OO   EE   IH   AY   U   O   EH   AH   AH

13. In our tradition the SHEH-HEH-CHEH-YAH-NOO is the prayer recited on the occasion of a happy experience. That you have learned to read Hebrew is such an occasion. This is a difficult prayer to read, do it slowly, but remember it well.

    בָּרוּךְ אַתָּה יְיָ אֱלֹהֵינוּ מֶלֶךְ הָעוֹלָם

    שֶׁהֶחֱיָנוּ וְקִיְּמָנוּ וְהִגִּיעָנוּ לַזְּמַן הַזֶה .

You've reached the end, and if you can read ALL of the words, on ALL of the Drill Sheets, you should be mighty proud of yourself.

ל	כ	י	ט	ח	ז	ו	ה	ד	ג	ב	א
30	20	10	9	8	7	6	5	4	3	2	1

ס	נ	מ
60	50	40

ת	ש	ר	ק	צ	פ	ע
400	300	200	100	90	80	70

1

פֶּסַח	לְסַדֵּר	סִדְרָה	סֵדֶר	סִדּוּר
Passover	to arrange	weekly portion	Seder	prayerbook

2

סִפּוּר	סִפְרִיָה	בֵּית סֵפֶר	סֵפֶר
story	library	school	book

3

לְסַפֵּר	סִינַי	נוֹסֵעַ	נִסִּים	נֵס
to tell	Sinai	travel	miracles	miracle

4

כְּנֶסֶת	סְפָרְדִי	סֻכּוֹת	סֻכָּה
Israeli Parliament	Spanish	Feast of Booths	Sukkah, booth

5

סְבִיבוֹן	אֶסְתֵּר	מַסֵכָה	כִּסֵא
dreidel	Esther	mask	chair

6

סוֹד	סְלִיחוֹת	סְלִיחָה	סִיוּם
secret	penitential prayers	Excuse me!	completion

7

סוֹף	יוֹסֵף	גוּף	אַף	כַּף	דַף
end	Joseph	body	nose	spoon	page

8

מַזָל טוֹב

Congratulations!

57

READING THAT FOLLOWS THE SH'MA BLESSING

You shall love the Lord, your God,	וְאָהַבְתָּ אֵת יְהוָֹה אֱלֹהֶיךָ	1
with all your heart	בְּכָל לְבָבְךָ	2
with all your soul,	וּבְכָל נַפְשְׁךָ	3
and with all your might.	וּבְכָל מְאֹדֶךָ	4
And these words	וְהָיוּ הַדְּבָרִים הָאֵלֶּה	5
which I command you this day	אֲשֶׁר אָנֹכִי מְצַוְּךָ הַיּוֹם	6
shall be upon your heart.	עַל לְבָבֶךָ.	7
You shall teach them diligently to your children,	וְשִׁנַּנְתָּם לְבָנֶיךָ	8
and shall speak of them	וְדִבַּרְתָּ בָּם	9
when you sit in your house,	בְּשִׁבְתְּךָ בְּבֵיתֶךָ	10
when you walk by the way,	וּבְלֶכְתְּךָ בַדֶּרֶךְ	11
when you lie down,	וּבְשָׁכְבְּךָ	12
and when you rise up.	וּבְקוּמֶךָ.	13
You shall bind them for a sign upon your hand	וּקְשַׁרְתָּם לְאוֹת עַל יָדֶךָ	14
and they shall be for frontlets between your eyes.	וְהָיוּ לְטֹטָפֹת בֵּין עֵינֶיךָ.	15
You shall write them upon the doorposts of your house	וּכְתַבְתָּם עַל מְזֻזוֹת בֵּיתֶךָ	16
and upon your gates.	וּבִשְׁעָרֶיךָ.	17
That you may remember	לְמַעַן תִּזְכְּרוּ	18
and do all My commandments	וַעֲשִׂיתֶם אֶת כָּל מִצְוֹתָי	19
and be holy unto your God.	וִהְיִיתֶם קְדֹשִׁים לֵאלֹהֵיכֶם.	20
I am the Lord your God.	אֲנִי יְהוָֹה אֱלֹהֵיכֶם.	21

Why is this night different	מַה נִּשְׁתַּנָּה הַלַּיְלָה הַזֶּה	1
from all other nights?	מִכָּל הַלֵּילוֹת?	2
For on all other nights we eat	שֶׁבְּכָל הַלֵּילוֹת אָנוּ אוֹכְלִין	3
either leavened or unleavened bread (mahtsah);	חָמֵץ וּמַצָּה	4
on this night (we eat) only unleavened bread.	הַלַּיְלָה הַזֶּה כֻּלּוֹ מַצָּה.	5
For on all other nights we eat	שֶׁבְּכָל הַלֵּילוֹת אָנוּ אוֹכְלִין	6
all kinds of herbs (green vegetables);	שְׁאָר יְרָקוֹת	7
on this night (we eat) bitter herbs (horse-radish).	הַלַּיְלָה הַזֶּה מָרוֹר.	8
For on all other nights we do not dip	שֶׁבְּכָל הַלֵּילוֹת אֵין אָנוּ מַטְבִּילִין	9
even one time;	אֲפִילוּ פַּעַם אֶחָת	10
on this night (we dip) two times.	הַלַּיְלָה הַזֶּה שְׁתֵּי פְעָמִים.	11
For on all other nights we eat	שֶׁבְּכָל הַלֵּילוֹת אָנוּ אוֹכְלִין	12
either sitting up or reclining (leaning);	בֵּין יוֹשְׁבִין וּבֵין מְסֻבִּין	13
on this night we all recline.	הַלַּיְלָה הַזֶּה כֻּלָּנוּ מְסֻבִּין.	14

HATIKVAH (The Hope)

1	כָּל עוֹד בַּלֵּבָב פְּנִימָה So long as within his heart
2	נֶפֶשׁ יְהוּדִי הוֹמִיָּה, The soul of the Jew longs,
3	וּלְפַאֲתֵי מִזְרָח קָדִימָה And he turns eastward,
4	עַיִן לְצִיּוֹן צוֹפִיָּה; His eye looking toward Zion,
5	עוֹד לֹא אָבְדָה תִקְוָתֵנוּ, Our hope is not yet lost.
6	הַתִּקְוָה שְׁנוֹת אַלְפַּיִם, The hope of two thousand years –
7	לִהְיוֹת עַם חָפְשִׁי בְּאַרְצֵנוּ, To be a free people in our land,
8	אֶרֶץ צִיּוֹן וִירוּשָׁלָיִם. The land of Zion and Jerusalem.

PRACTICE IN WRITING SCRIPT

So far, you have made all of your Hebrew letters in block form. But there is another form for the Hebrew alphabet, too. When people write to one another in the Hebrew language, they usually use a form of script writing which we call *cursive.* In the next few pages you can practice drawing Hebrew in cursive letters. So that the new cursive form will not be strange to you, copy the chart on the following page into your Hebrew notebook and refer to it as you practice the art of writing in Hebrew.

אָלֶף בֵּית
HEBREW ALPHABET

N̦	M	מ מ		*IƆ̦*	Silent	א א
Ṗ	Final M	ם ם		*ב̦*	B	בּ ב
JJ	N	נ נ		*ב̦*	V	ב ב
I	Final N	ן ן		*ג̦*	(get) G	ג ג
IQ̦	S	ס ס		*ז̦*	D	ד ד
ƺ	Silent	ע ע		*ה̦*	H	ה ה
פ̦	P	פּ פ		*I*	V	ו ו
פ̦	F	פ פ		*h̦*	Z	ז ז
ƽ	Final F	ף ף		*ח̦*	CH	ח ח
3	TS	צ צ		*ט̦*	T	ט ט
ƽ	Final TS	ץ ץ		*I*	Y	י י
ק̦	K	ק ק		*ɔ̦*	K	כּ כ
ר̦	R	ר ר		*ɔ*	CH	כ כ
ש̦	SH	שׁ שׁ		*ר̦*	Final Ḥ	ך ך
ש̦	S	שׂ שׂ		*ƽ*	L	ל ל
ת̦	T	תּ תּ				
ת̦	T	ת ת				

Note: In writing, begin each letter where you see the number 1. Then follow the arrows.

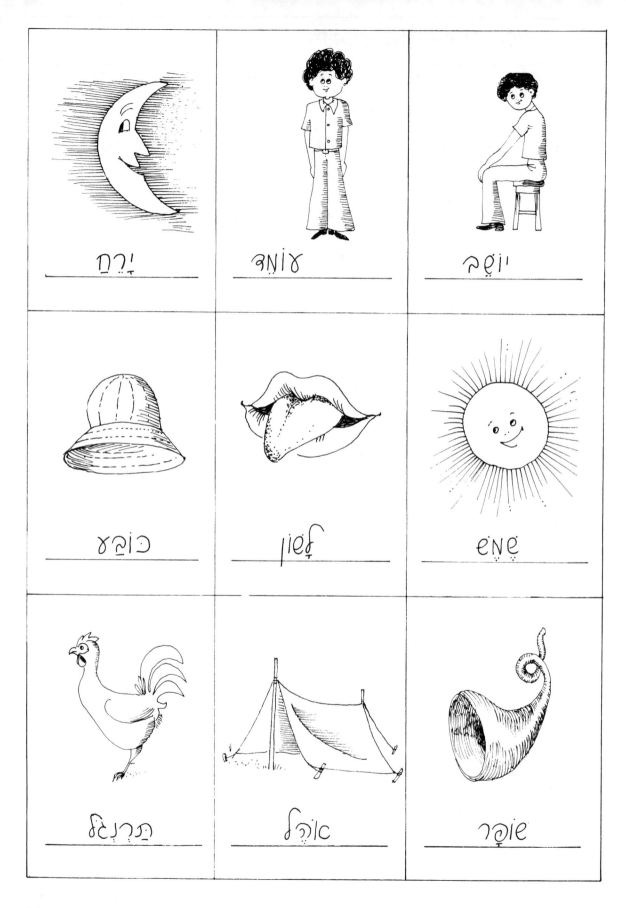

יָרֵחַ	עוֹמֵד	יוֹשֵׁב
כּוֹבַע	שָׂפָם	שֶׁמֶשׁ
תַּרְנְגוֹל	אוֹהֶל	שׁוֹפָר

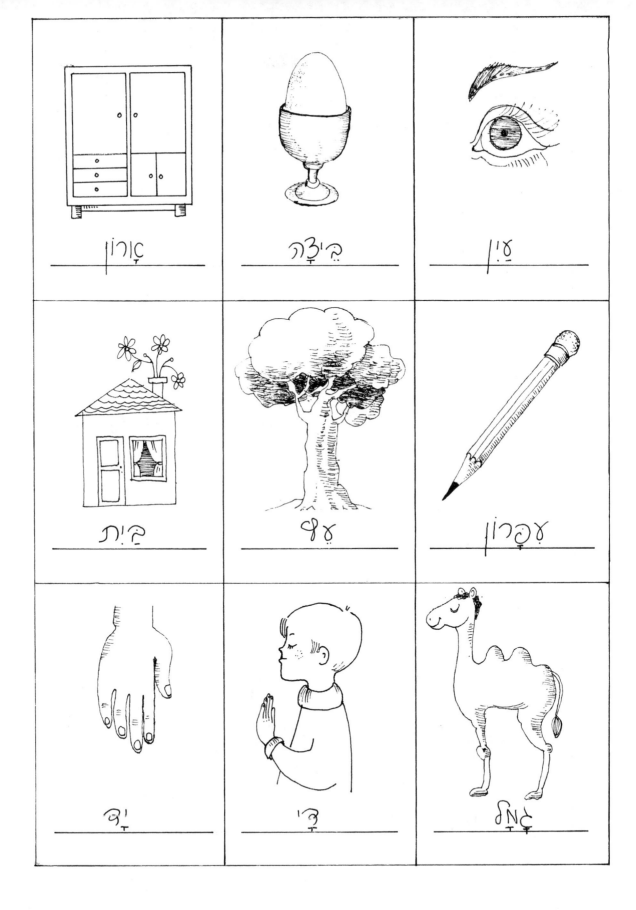

אַרְגּוֹן	בֵּיצָה	עַיִן
בַּיִת	עֵץ	עִפָּרוֹן
יָד	יֶלֶד	גָּמָל

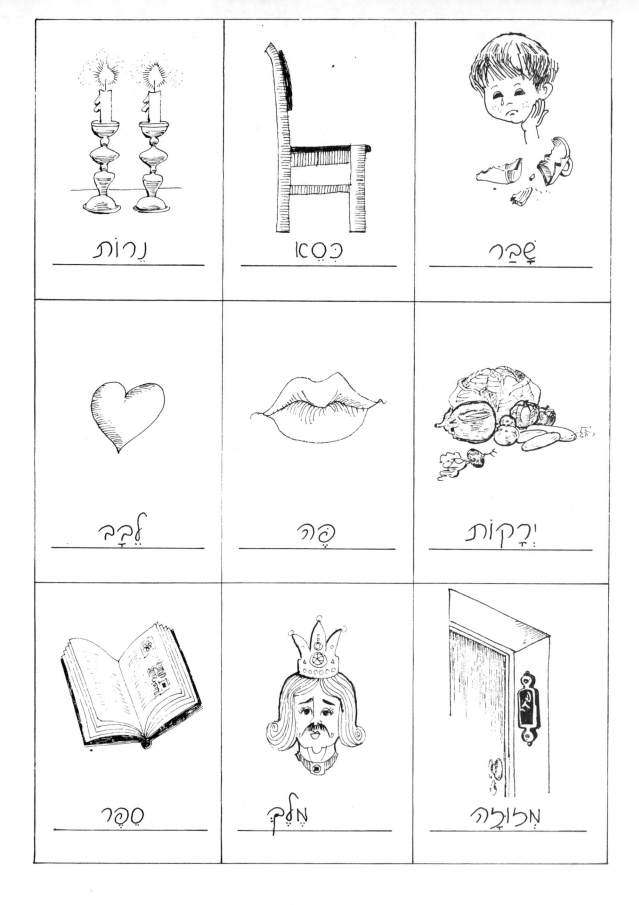

נֵרוֹת	כִּסֵּא	שָׁבַר
לֵבָב	פֶּה	יְרָקוֹת
סֵפֶר	מֶלֶךְ	מְזוּזָה